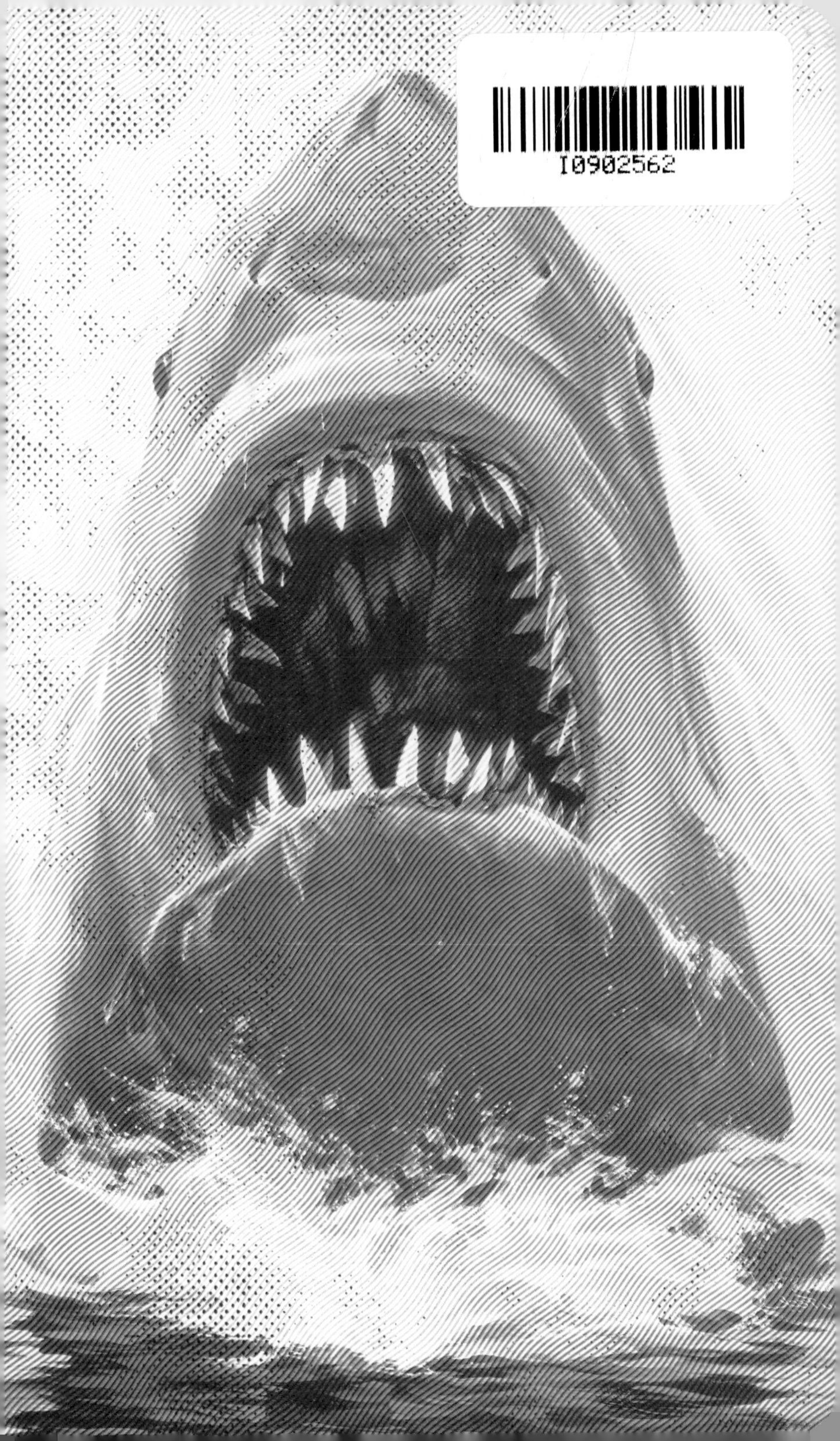

YOU'RE GONNA NEED A

Bigger

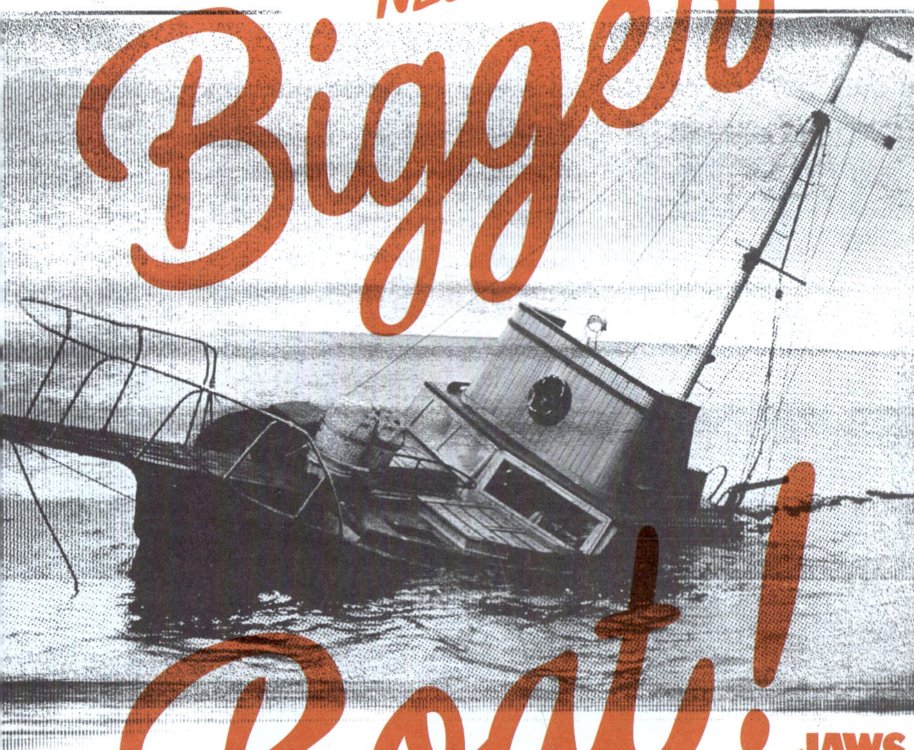

Boat!

JAWS

AMITY 1975

THIS BELONGS TO

____

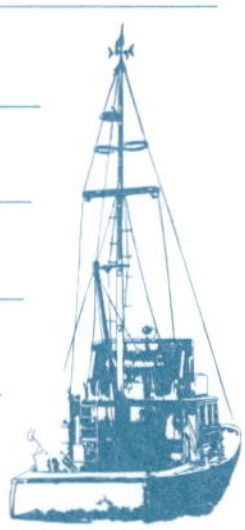

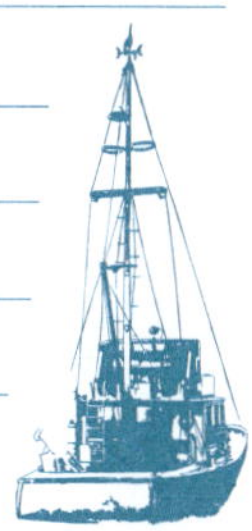

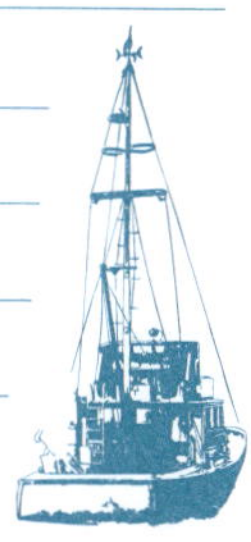

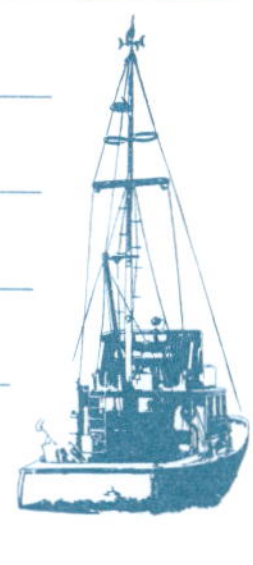

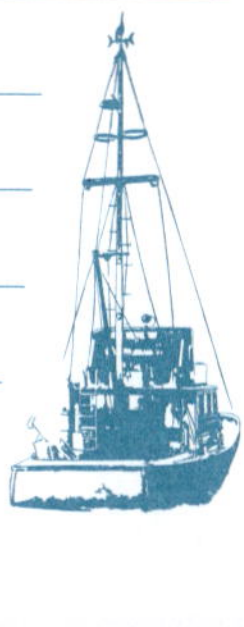

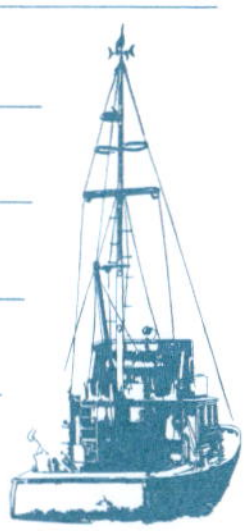

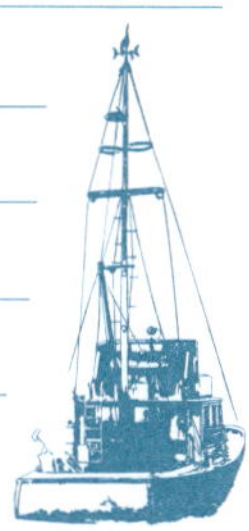

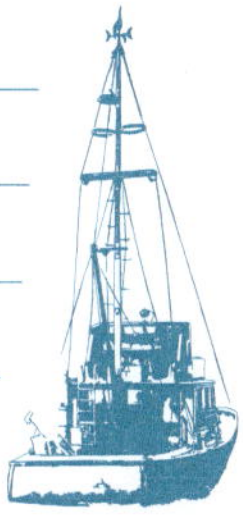

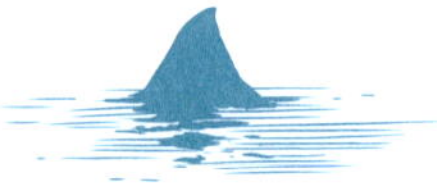

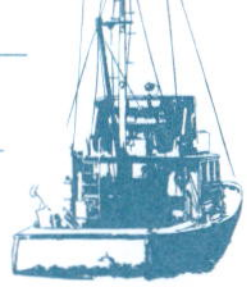

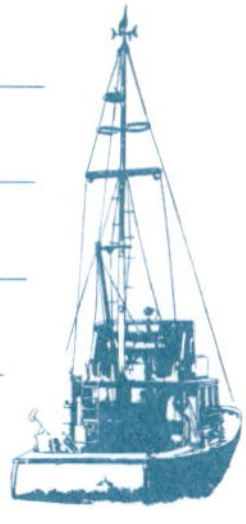

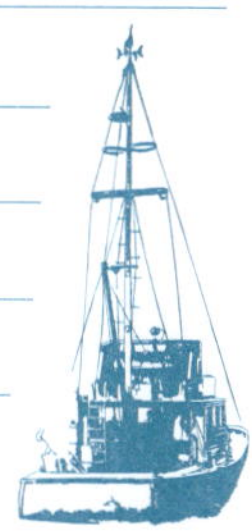

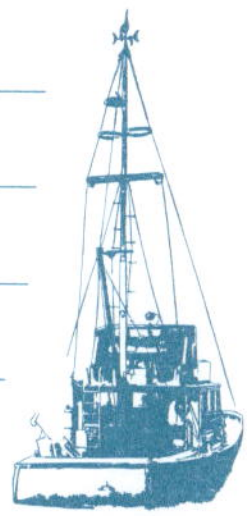

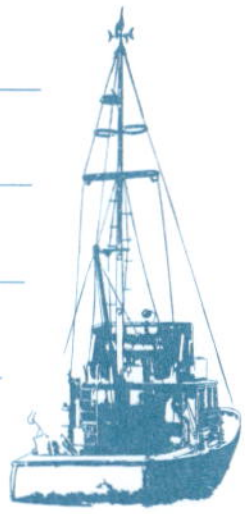

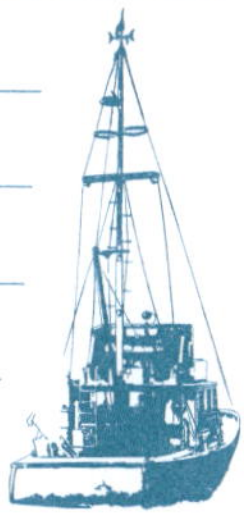

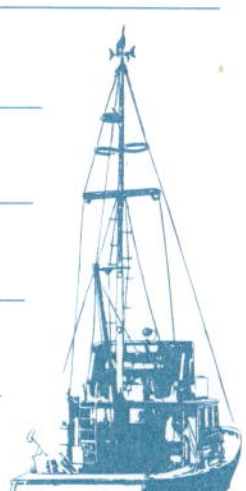

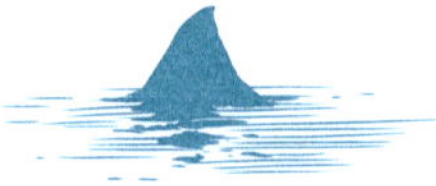

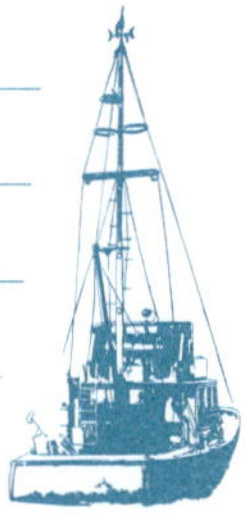

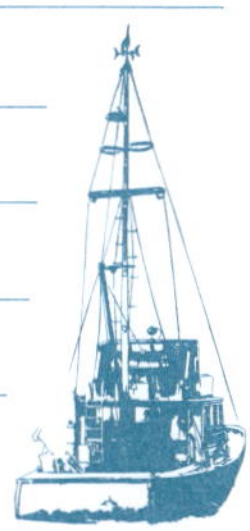

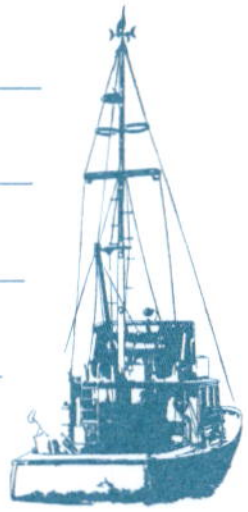

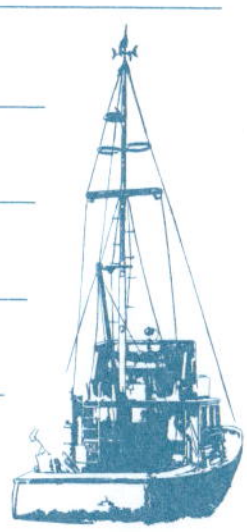

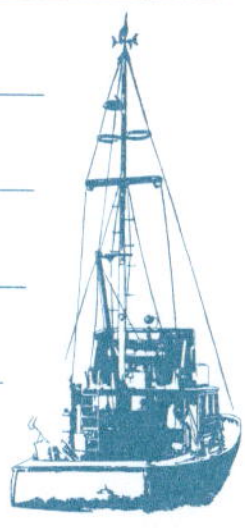

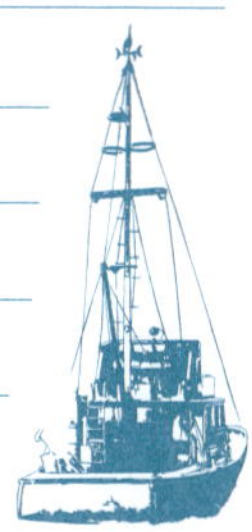

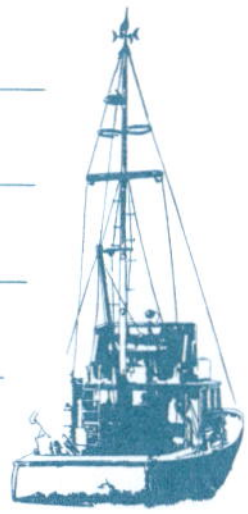

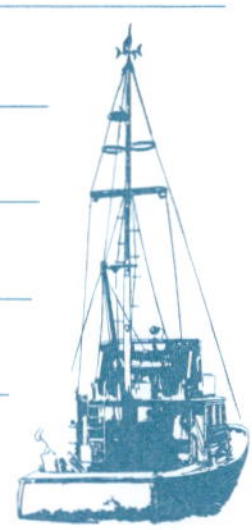

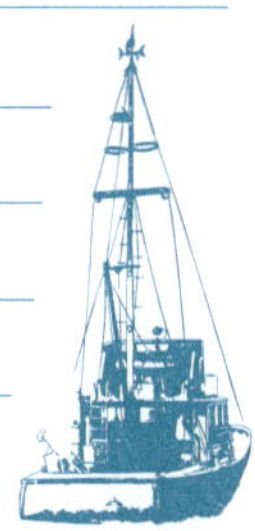

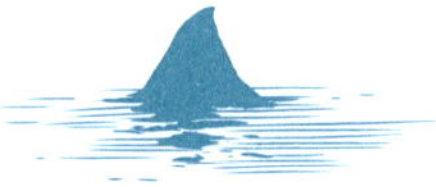

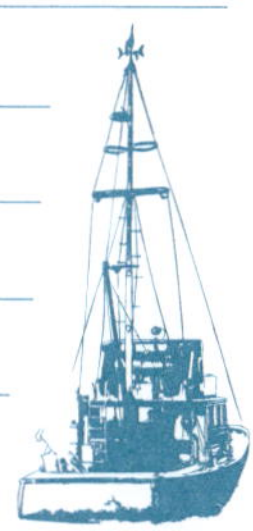

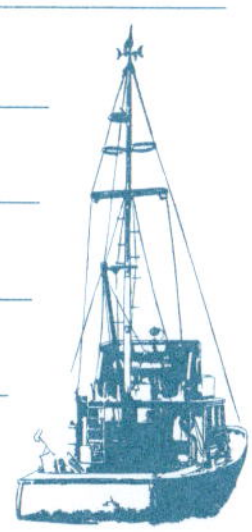

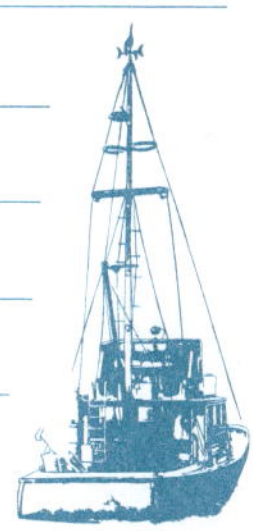

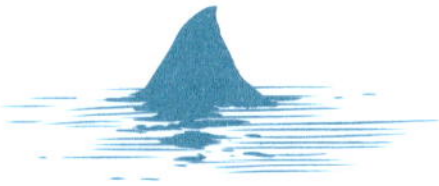

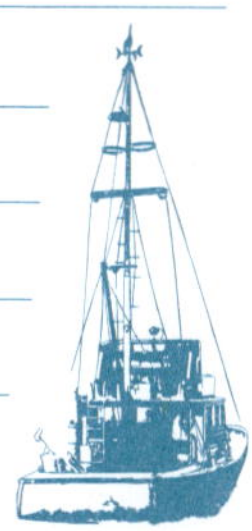

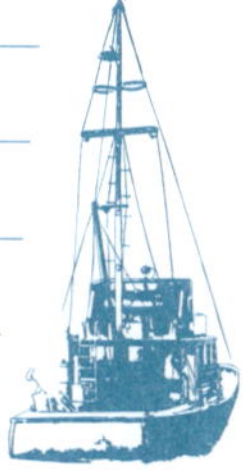

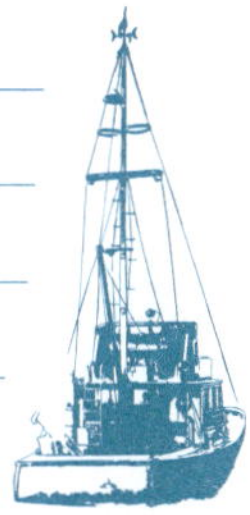

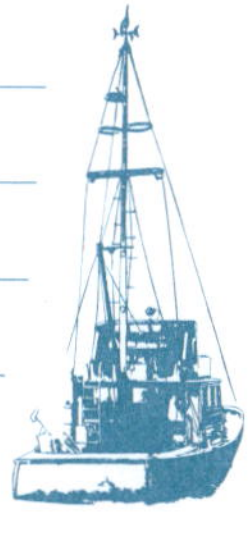

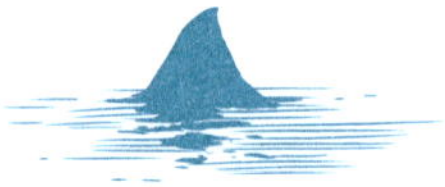

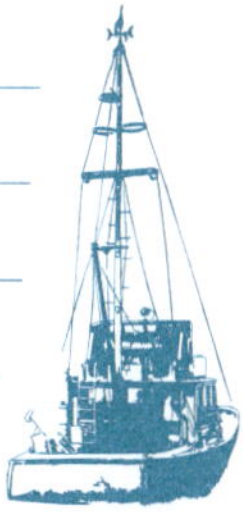

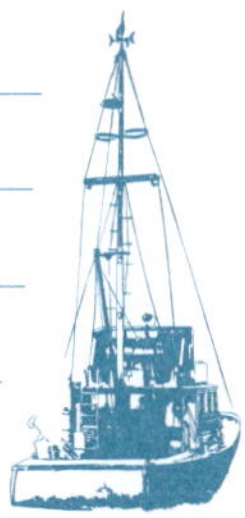

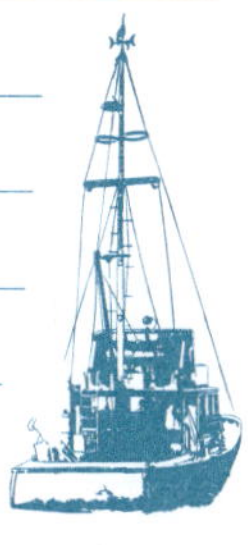

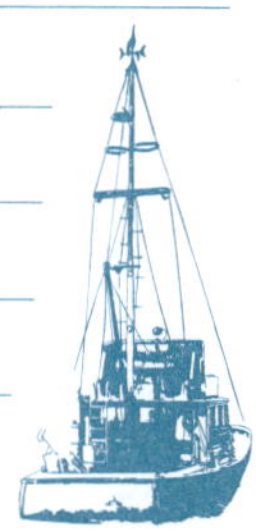

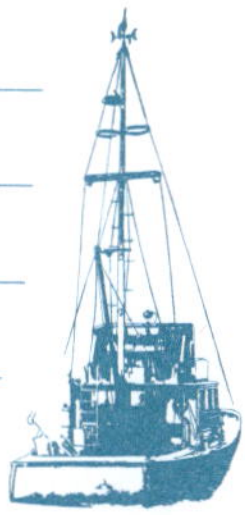

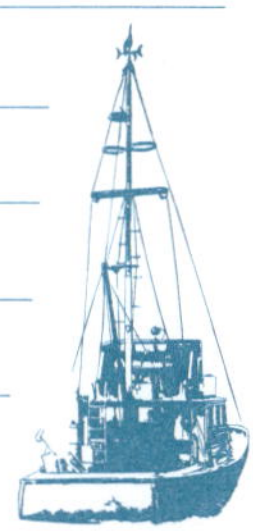

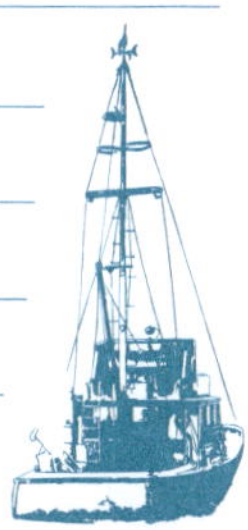

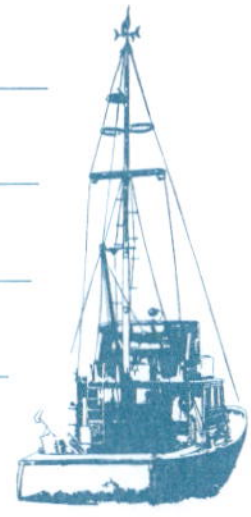

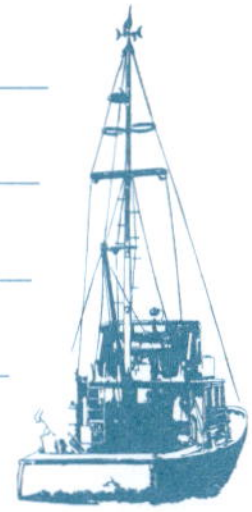

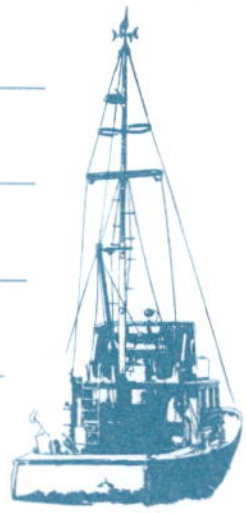

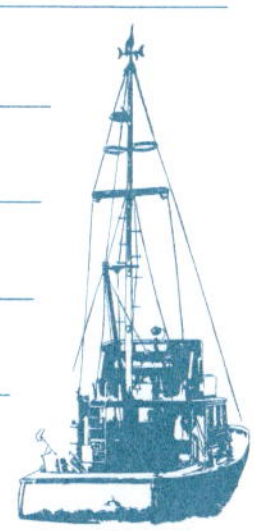

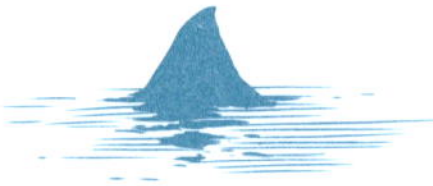

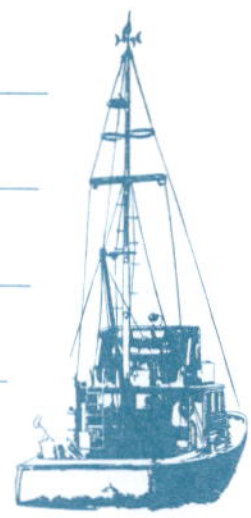

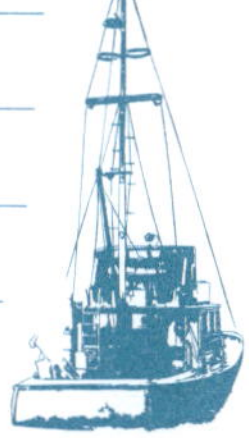

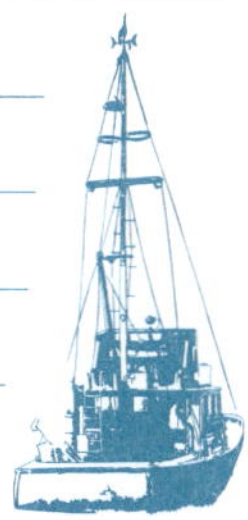

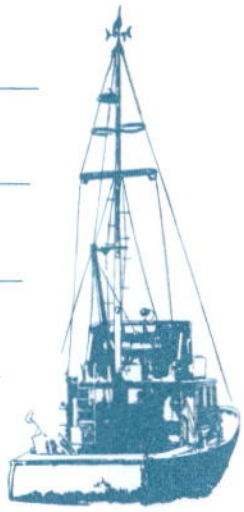

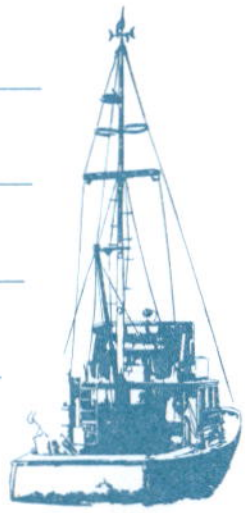

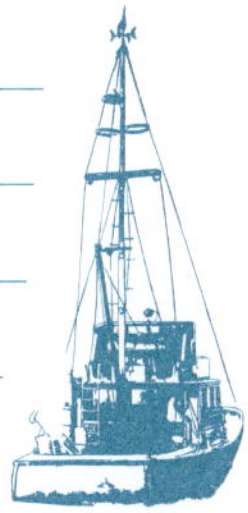

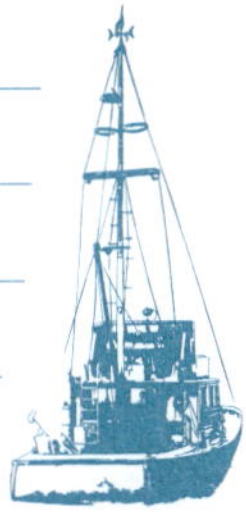

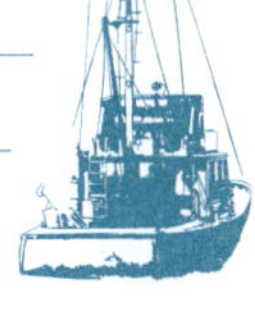

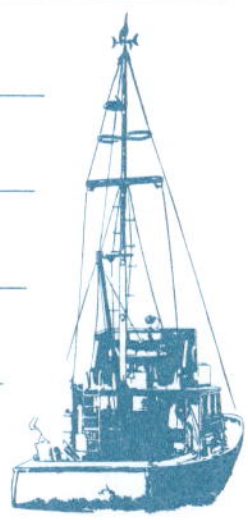

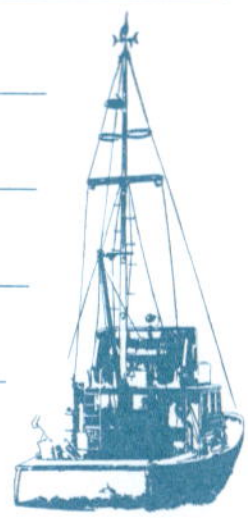

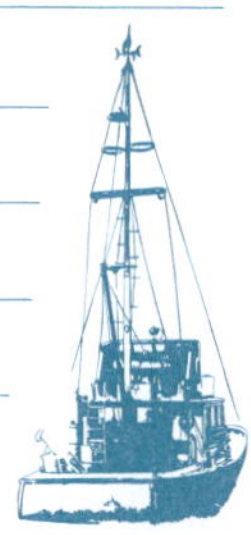

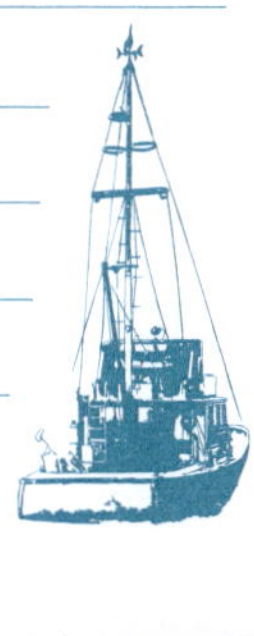

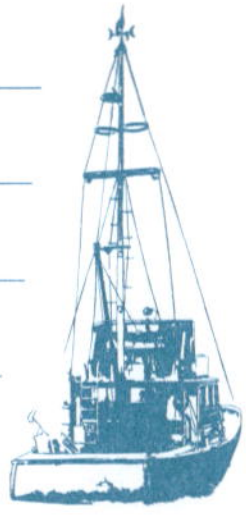

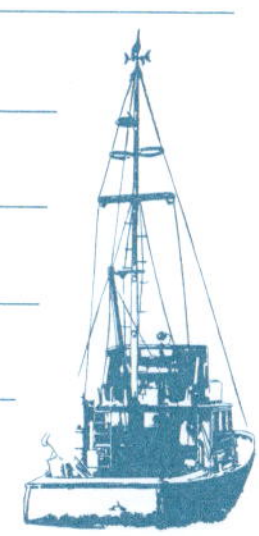

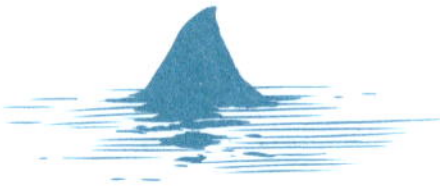

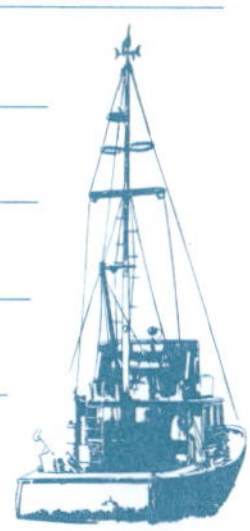

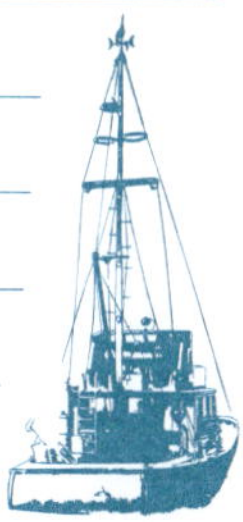

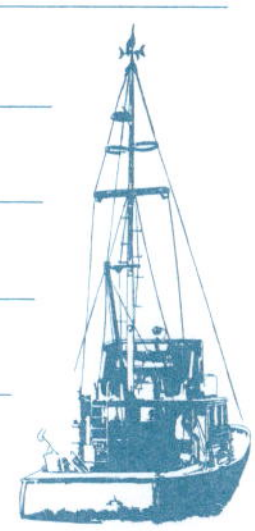

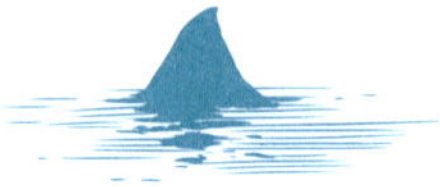

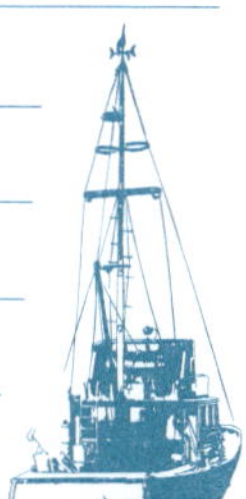

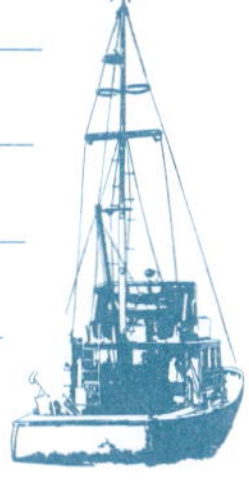

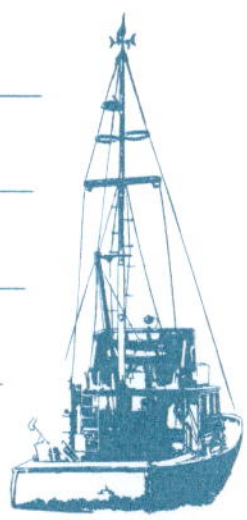

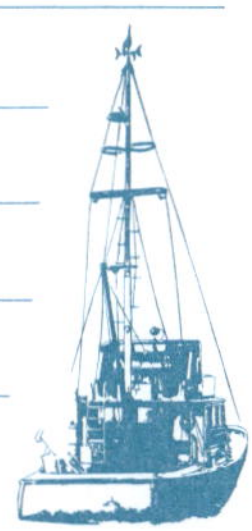

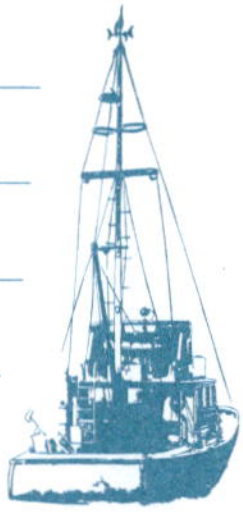

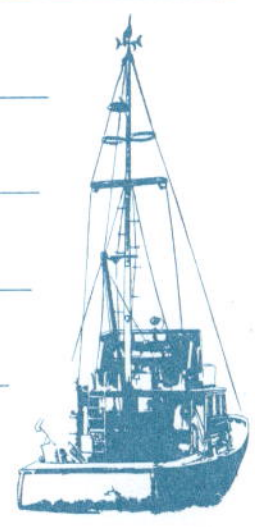

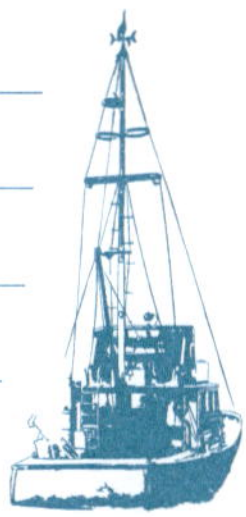

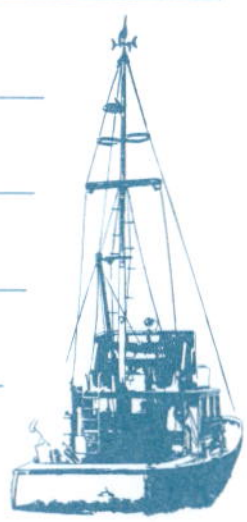

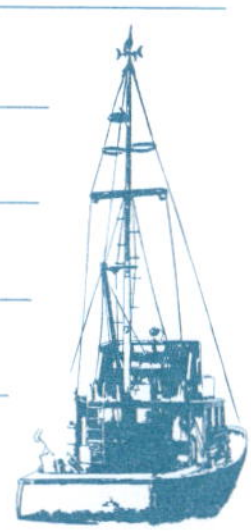

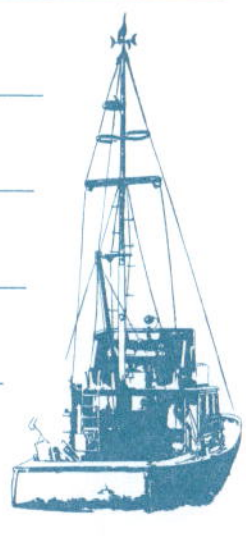

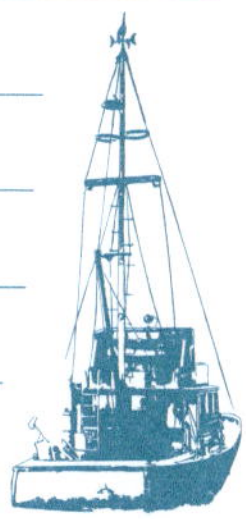

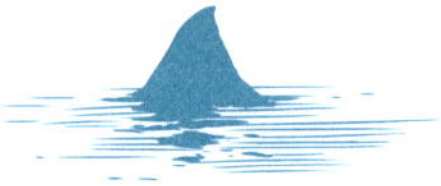

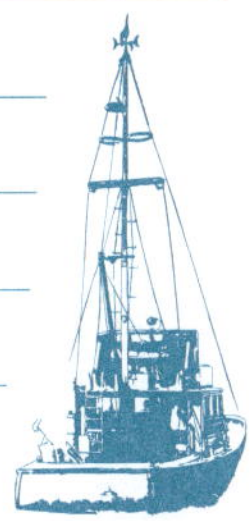

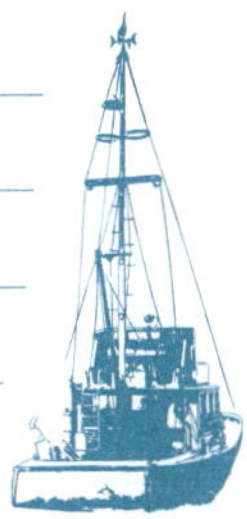

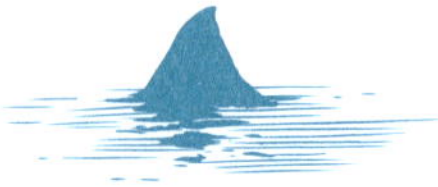

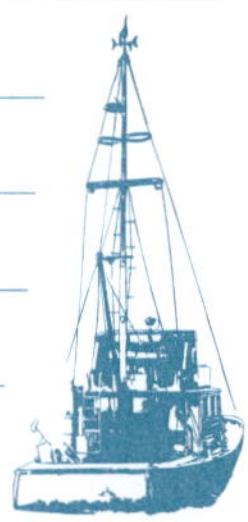

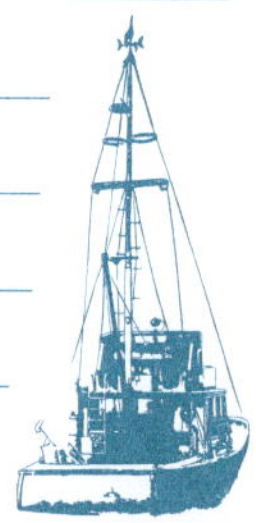

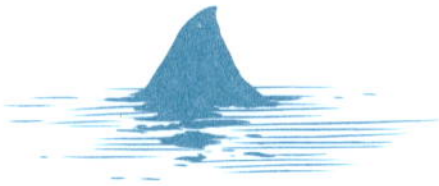

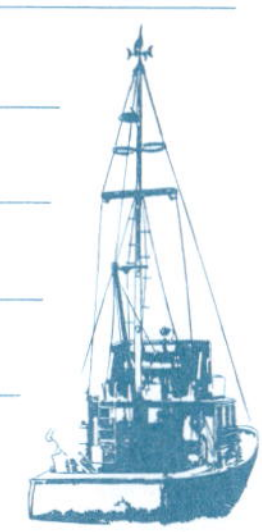

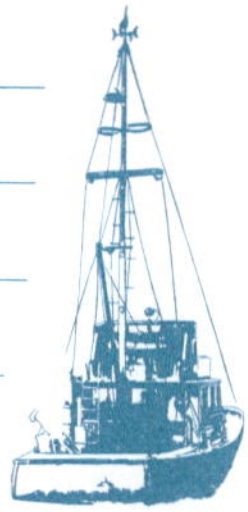

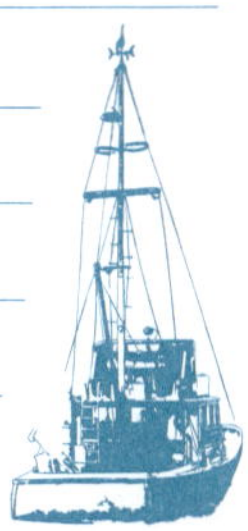

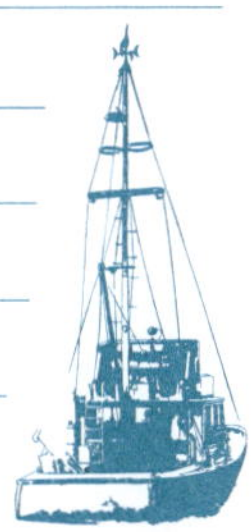

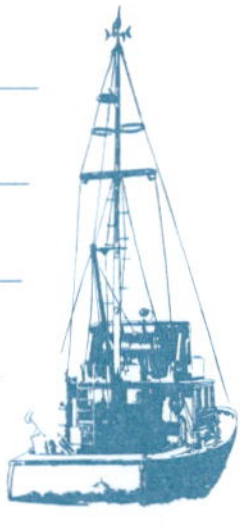

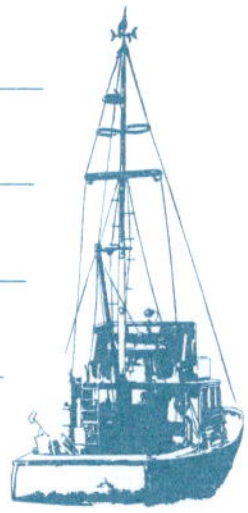

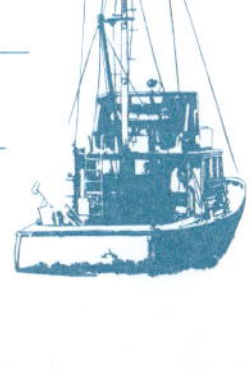

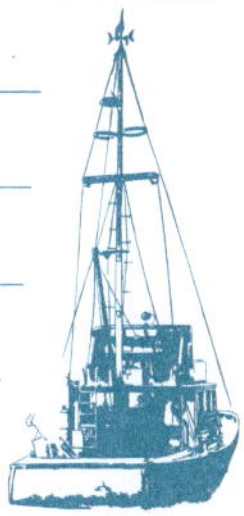

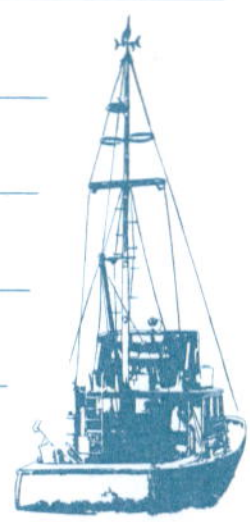

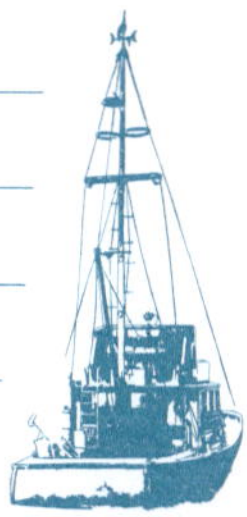

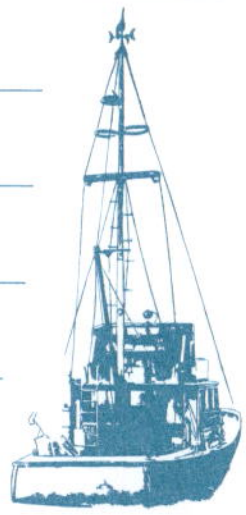

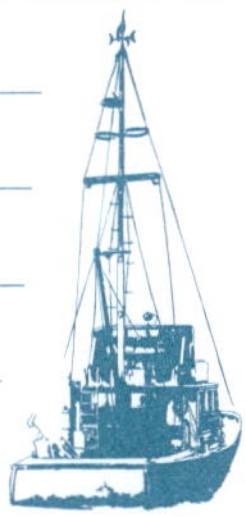

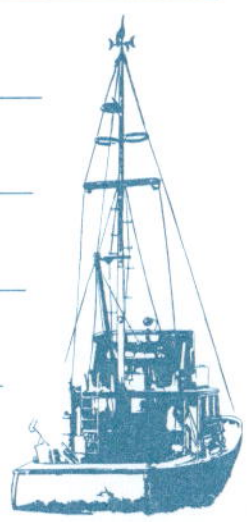

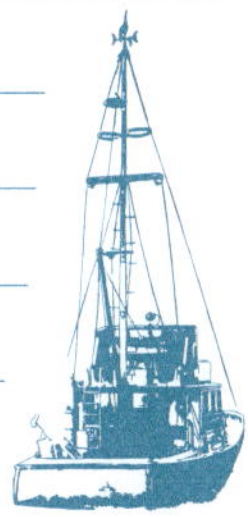

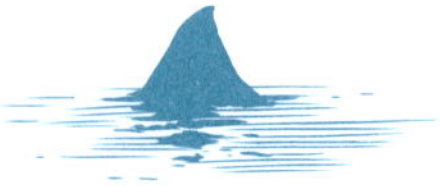

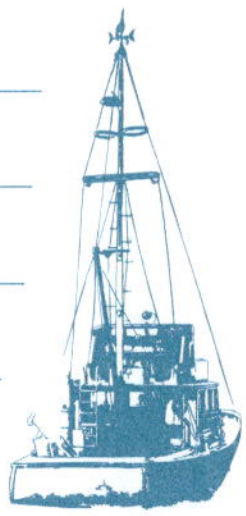

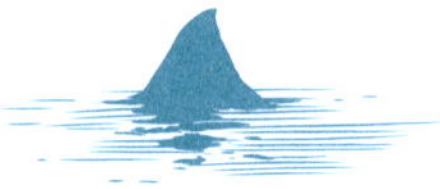

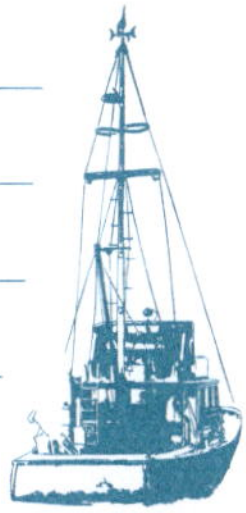

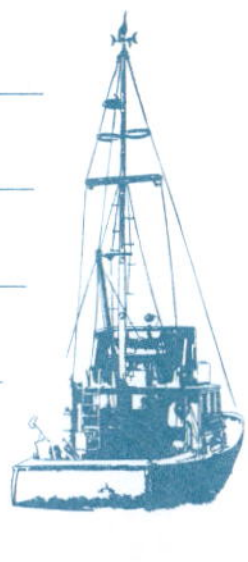

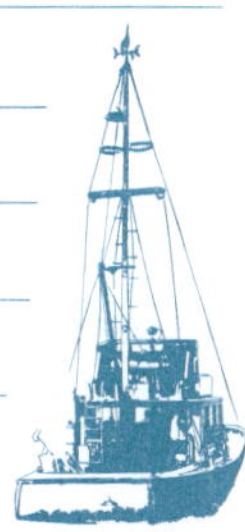

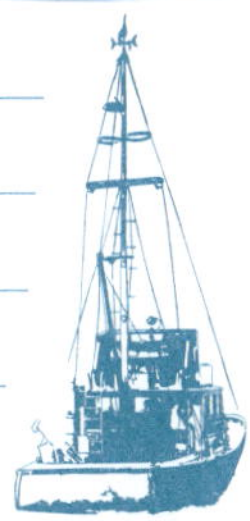

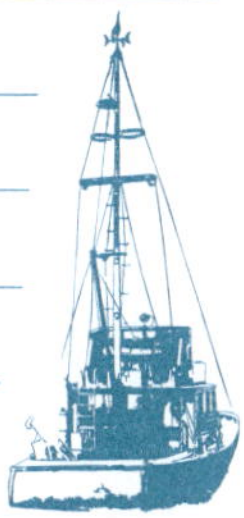

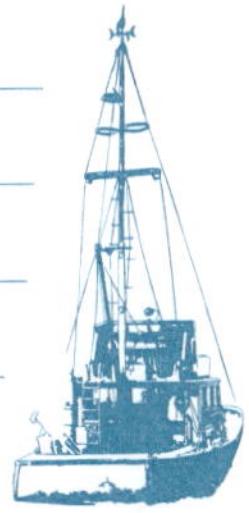

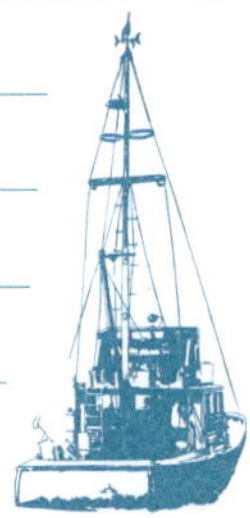

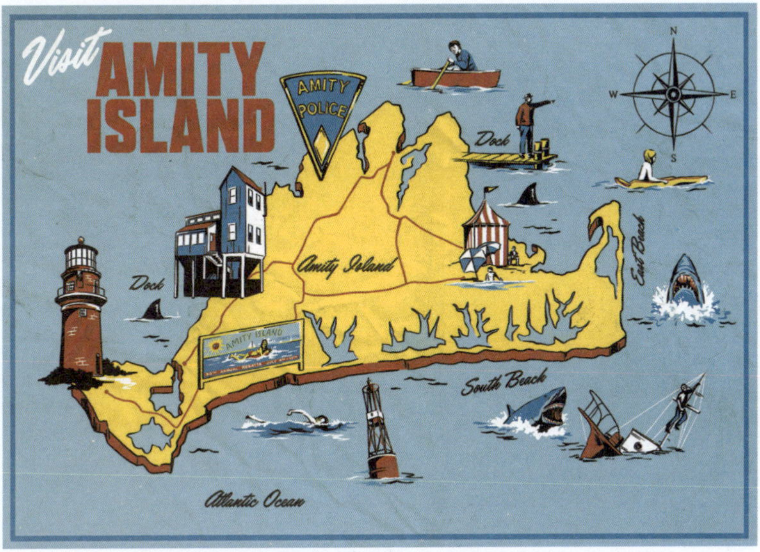

insighteditions.com

Manufactured in China

10 9 8 7 6 5 4 3 2 1

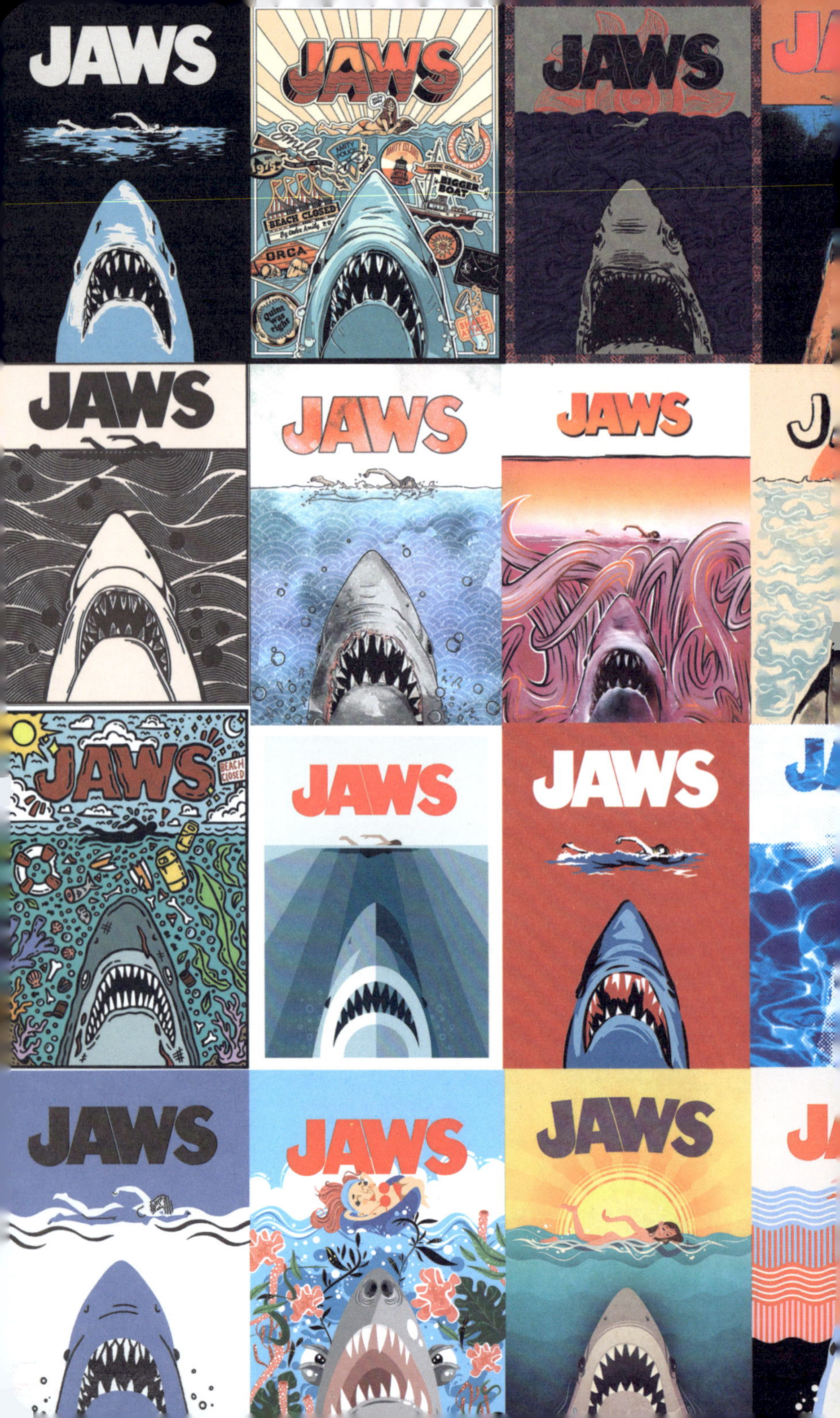
JAWS
JAWS
Smile
AMITY ISLAND
BIGGER BOAT
BEACH CLOSED
ORCA
Quint was right
SHARK ATTACK
JAWS
JAWS
JAWS
JAWS
JAWS
BEACH CLOSED
JAWS
JAWS
JAWS
JAWS
JAWS